The Notebook
Pocket Edition

I0146160

Chasing Horses

2021

The Notebook: Pocket Edition A reference manual to help you document the wild horse herd living wild and free in Theodore Roosevelt National Park
ISBN: 978-1-7322720-7-1
Published 2021 by Chasing Horses 312 Pacific Ave, Medora, ND 58645
e-mail:imchasinghorses@gmail.com
website: www.chasinghorses.com
Text and images copyright © Christine and Gary Kman
The Notebook is self-published by Chasing Horses
First Edition Book Design by Christine Kman
Text and photographs by Christine and Gary Kman

Hello and welcome to The Notebook ~ Pocket Edition!

We heard you when you asked for a book that you could take along with you in the park and carry easily to help identify the horses you find. We hope you enjoy the 2021 edition!

The purpose of this book is simply to help you identify the horses. The book is separated by band with a list of all of the horses in that band (as of February 2021) and a photo of each horse in the band with their name listed under their photo.

The full version of The Notebook shares a lot more information and stories. If you don't have your copy yet, you can stop in our shop in Medora, ND and pick one up, or you can visit our website at www.chasinghorses.com and order yours today!

We hope you enjoy this book. More than any-thing, we hope it helps you while you are out....

Thank you for your support!
Chris & Gary
www.chasing

Chasing Horses

Please note:

The horses change colors during the
seasons. This may cause them to look
different depending on the time of the year you
visit.

Stallion Arrowhead's Band

o Stallion Arrowhead
o Mare Little Brother's Girl
o Mare Diamond
o Mare Domino
o Mare Blue
o Mare Papoose
o Mare Justice
o Mare Velvet
o Mare Opal
o Filly Antice
o Filly Frosted Arrow
o Filly Betsy
o Colt Blackjack

Chasing Horses
Notes

Stallion Arrowhead

Mare Little Brother's Girl

Mare Diamond

Mare Domino

Mare Blue

Mare Papoose

Mare Justice

Mare Velvet

Mare Opal

Filly Antice

Filly Frosted Arrow

Colt Blackjack

Filly Betsy

Stallion Coal's Band

o Stallion Coal

o Mare Busy Blue

o Mare Betty Blue

o Mare Maggie

o Mare Dixie

o Colt Amantes

Chasing Horses
NOTES

Stallion Coal

Mare Busy Blue

Mare Betty Blue

Colt Amantes

Mare Dixie

Mare Maggie

Stallion Copper's Band

o Stallion Copper

o Mare Daisy

o Mare Esprit

o Mare Juniper

o Mare Faith

o Mare Grace

Filly Belle

Chasing Horses
NOTES

Stallion Copper

Mare Daisy

Mare Esprit

Mare Juniper

Mare Faith

Mare Grace

Filly Belle

Stallion Flax's Band

o Stallion Flax

o Mare Dolly

o Mare Mischief

o Mare Kat

o Filly Amargo

o Colt Anzar

o Mare Firefly

o Mare Smokie

o Mare Paience

o Filly Anuk

o Filly Bird

o Colt Bokel

o Filly Bluff

Chasing Horses
NOTES

Stallion Flax

Mare Dolly

Mare Mischief

Mare Kat

Filly Amargo

Colt Anzar

Mare Firefly

Mare Smokie

Mare Patience

Filly Bluff

Filly Anuk

Colt Bokel

Filly Bird

Stallion Georgia's Boy's Band

o Stallion Georgia's Boy

o Mare Flicka

o Mare Shale

o Mare Whiskey

o Mare Vicki

o Mare Holly

o Filly Noelle

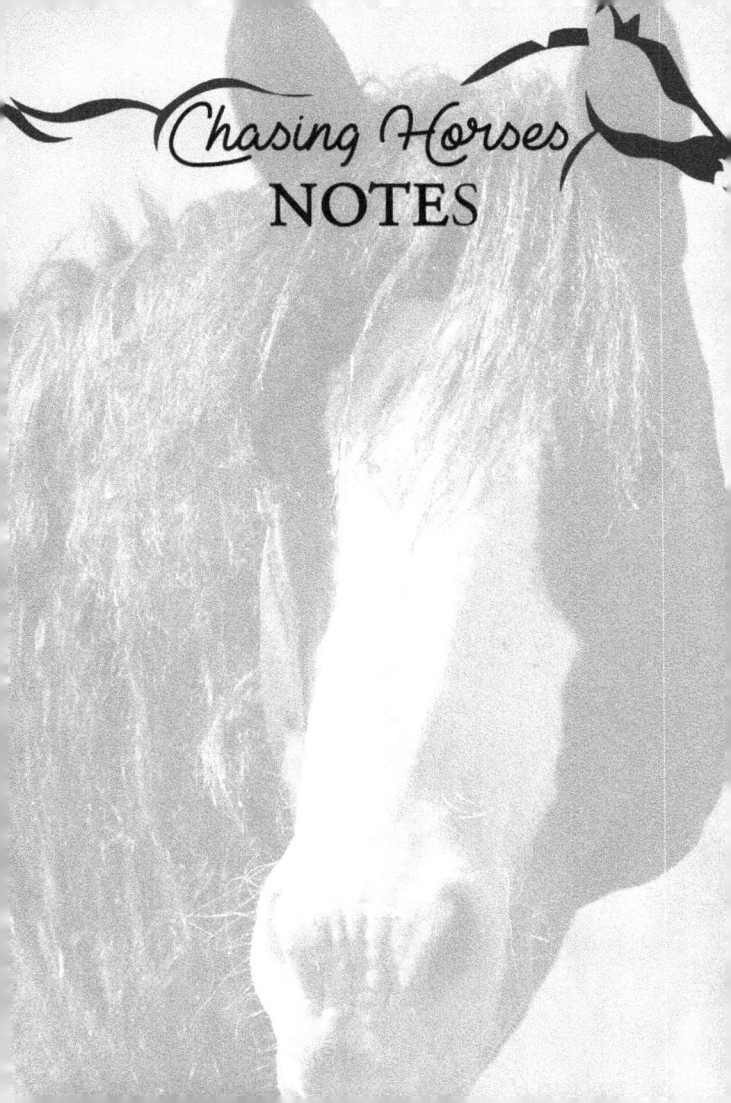

Chasing Horses
NOTES

Stallion Georgia's Boy

Mare Flicka

Mare
Shale

Mare Whiskey

Mare Vicki

Mare Holly

Filly Noelle

Stallion Grady's Band

o Stallion Grady

o Mare Blondie

o Mare Twister

o Mare Quinn

o Colt Arcola

o Filly Bonnet

o Colt Anthem

o Colt Blazo

Chasing Horses
NOTES

Stallion Grady

Mare Blondie

Mare Twister

Mare Quinn

Colt Arcola

Filly Bonnet

Colt Anthem

Colt Blazo

Stallion Guardian's Band

oStallion Guardian

oMare Freckles

oFilly Katie

Chasing Horses
NOTES

Stallion Guardian

Mare Freckles

Filly Katie

Stallion Gunner's Band

- Stallion Gunner
- Mare Perdita
- Filly Anisak
- Filly Birch
- Filly Anisak
- Mare Sundance
- Filly Raven
- Mare Cedar
- Filly Raven's Myst
- Filly Mystique

Chasing Horses
NOTES

Stallion Gunner

Mare Perdita

Filly Anisak

Filly Birch

Mare
Sundance

Mare Cedar

Mare Raven

Filly Raven's Myst

2021 Filly Mystique
(Raven x Mystery)

Stallion Half Moon's Band

- Stallion Half Moon
- Mare Tanker
- Mare Rosie
- Mare Punkin
- Mare Eclipse
- Mare Sumac
- Colt Aloe
- Filly Bea
- Filly Star

Chasing Horses

NOTES

Stallion Half Moon

Mare Tanker

Mare Rosie

Mare Sumac

Mare Eclipse

Colt Aloe

Filly Bea

Filly Star

Stallion Ollie Jr.'s Band

o Stallion Ollie Jr.

o Mare Sapphire

o Mare Stormy

o Mare Autumn

o Filly Aqua

o Colt Applewood

o Filly Pixie

o Filly Bess

o Filly Jewel

Chasing Horses
NOTES

Stallion Ollie Jr.

Mare Sapphire

Mare Stormy

Mare Autumn

Colt
Applewood

Filly Aqua

Filly Pixie

Filly Bess

Filly Jewel

Stallion Red Face's Band

- Stallion Red Face
- Mare Frosty
- Mare Flame
- Mare Pretty Girl
- Mare Lakota
- Mare Emmylou
- Mare Ember's Girl
- Mare Eagle
- Filly Emery
- Filly Birdie
- Colt Banty
- Filly Little Mo

Stallion Red Face

Mare Frosty

Mare
Flame

Mare Pretty Girl

Mare Lakota

Mare Emmylou

Mare Ember's Girl

Mare Eagle

Filly Emery

Filly Birdie

Colt Banty

Filly Little Mo

Stallion Remington's Band

- Stallion Remington
- Mare Democracy
- Mare Ardena
- Colt Bart

Stallion Remington

Mare Democracy

Mare Ardena

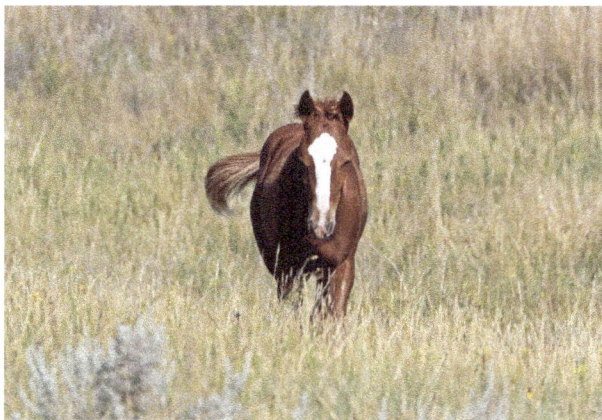

Colt Bart

Stallion Satellite's Band

- Stallion Satellite
- Mare Lightening
- Mare Crow
- Mare Minnie
- Filly Almanac
- Filly Little Bear

Stallion Satellite

Mare Lightening

Mare Crow

Mare Minnie

Filly Almanac

Filly
Little
Bear

Stallion Sidekick's Band

o Stallion Sidekick

o Mare Bella

o Mare Mist

o Mare Maiden

o Mare River

o Mare Snip's Gray

o Mare Valentina

o Mare Escape

o Filly Misty Blue

o Filly Bayou

o Filly Annabella

Chasing Horses
NOTES

Stallion Sidekick

Mare Bella

Mare Mist

Mare River

Mare Maiden

Mare Escape

Snip's Gray

Mare
Valentina

Filly
Misty
Blue

Filly Bayou

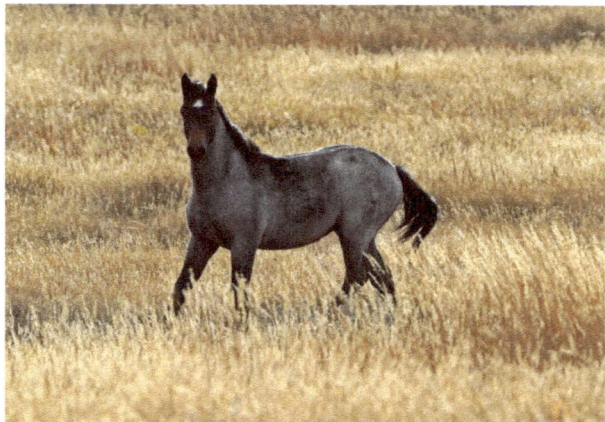

Filly Annabella

Stallion Teton's Band

o Stallion Teton

o Mare Ruby

o Mare Goblin

o Mare TeePee

o Mare Indian Paint Brush

o Mare June

o Colt Alluvium

o Colt Apex

o Filly Archer

o Filly Bee

o Filly Shayna

o Filly Berkleigh

o Filly Bonanza

Chasing Horses
NOTES

Stallion Teton

Mare Ruby

Mare Goblin

Mare TeePee

Mare
Indian
Paint
Brush

Mare June

Colt Apex

Filly Archer

Colt
Alluvium

Filly Bee

Filly Shayna

Filly
Berkleigh

Colt
Bonanza

Stallion Trooper's Band

- Stallion Trooper
- Mare Maddie
- Mare Cassie
- Mare Dawn
- Mare Penny
- Mare Paisley
- Mare Patches
- Mare Skipper
- Mare Aurora
- Colt Arey
- Filly Bluegrass

Chasing Horses
NOTES

Stallion Trooper

Mare Maddie

Mare Cassie

Mare Penny

Mare Skipper

Mare Dawn

Mare Paisley

Mare
Patches

Mare Aurora

Colt
Arey

Filly Bluegrass

Stallion Wild Rye's Band

- oStallion Wild Rye
- oMare Little Gray
- oMare Paige
- oMare Lorena
- oFilly Pippi
- oFilly Lorelye

Chasing Horses
NOTES

Stallion Wild Rye

Mare Paige

Mare
Lorena

Mare Little Gray

Filly Pippi

Filly Lorelye

Stallion Xander's Band

o Stallion Xander

o Mare Pale Lady

o Mare Winter

o Mare Angel

o Mare Spotted Blue

o Mare Cowgirl

o Mare Taylor

o Colt Amite

o Filly Blue Angel

o Colt Boomer

Chasing Horses
NOTES

Stallion
Xander

Mare Pale Lady

Mare Winter

Mare Spotted Blue

Mare Angel

Mare Cowgirl

Mare Taylor

Filly
Blue
Angel

Colt
Amite

Colt
Boomer

The Bachelor Stallions

oStallion Circus
oStallion Cloud
oStallion Brutus
oStallion Maverick
oStallion Nicols
oStallion Frontier
oStallion Yoakum
oStallion Flash
oStallion Illinois
oStallion Thunder Cloud
oStallion Cagney

Chasing Horses
NOTES

Stallion Circus

Stallion Cloud

Stallion Brutus

Stallion Maverick

Stallion Frontier

Stallion Thunder Cloud

Stallion Nicols

Stallion Yoakum

Stallion
Flash

Stallion Illinois

Stallion Cagney

Chasing Horses

NOTES

Chasing Horses
NOTES

Chasing Horses
NOTES

Want more?

Stay up to date on what happens next
with the wild horses of
Theodore Roosevelt National Park
by following us on Facebook & Instagram

Thank you for your support!
www.chasinghorses.com

www.ingramcontent.com/pod-product-compliance
Lightning Source LLC
Chambersburg PA
CBHW041221030426
42336CB00024B/3408